SPOTLIGHT ON
CIVIC COURAGE
HEROES OF CONSCIENCE™

MAHATMA GANDHI

CHAMPION OF INDIAN INDEPENDENCE

Monique Vescia

Rosen
YA™

New York

Published in 2018 by The Rosen Publishing Group, Inc.
29 East 21st Street, New York, NY 10010

Library of Congress Cataloging-in-Publication Data

Names: Vescia, Monique.
Title: Mahatma Gandhi: champion of Indian independence / Monique Vescia.
Description: First edition. | New York : Rosen YA, [2018] | Series: Spotlight on civic courage : heroes of conscience | Includes bibliographical references and index. | Audience: Grades 5–10.
Identifiers: LCCN 2017011644| ISBN 9781538380864 (library bound) | ISBN 9781538380833 (pbk.) | ISBN 9781538380840 (6 pack)
Subjects: LCSH: Gandhi, Mahatma, 1869–1948—Juvenile literature. | Statesmen—India—Biography—Juvenile literature. | Nationalists—India—Biography—Juvenile literature.
Classification: LCC DS481.G3 V48 2018 | DDC 954.03/5092 [B] —dc23
LC record available at https://lccn.loc.gov/2017011644

Manufactured in the United States of America

On the cover: This photo of Gandhi dates from around 1940. The photo in the background shows a march supporting a boycott against British goods that took place in Bombay, India, in 1930 and was part of the movement for Indian independence that Gandhi led.

CONTENTS

A GREAT SOUL

The man who would one day become known as the Mahatma, or "great soul," and be compared to Buddha and Jesus Christ did not begin life in a very promising way. A fearful child and a mediocre student, he suffered from extreme shyness and depression. Raised in a vegetarian family, he ate meat in secret and once stole a statue from a temple.

Yet Mohandas Gandhi would eventually transform himself into a formidable spiritual and political leader. His devotion to truth and his capacity for self-sacrifice earned him the respect of his opponents and helped gain India its independence from British rule. As early as 1919, the British scholar Gilbert Murray warned those in power they should "be very careful how they deal with a man who cares ... nothing for riches, nothing for comfort or praise, or promotion, but is simply determined to do what he believes to be right."

Underestimated by many, Mohandas Gandhi became an effective and inspiring leader. He would challenge the power of the mighty British Empire.

THE TIMID CHILD

Mohandas Karamchand Gandhi was born in Porbandar, India, on October 2, 1869. His father was the *diwan*, or political leader, of that coastal city. The Gandhi family belonged to the Vaishya caste and observed traditions from both the Hindu religion and Jainism. His mother's deep religious devotion made a strong impression on Mohandas.

The youngest child in a large family, Mohan, as he was called, was a timid boy. Snakes, thieves, and ghosts all frightened him, and he had a terror of the dark. Mohan was also painfully shy. He spent much of his time reading and studying, though he was just an average student. Like many adolescents, he went through a rebellious period during which he broke rules.

Hindu families traditionally arranged marriages for their children. At age thirteen, Mohan married a girl named Kasturba, a young bride his parents had chosen for him. Eventually, the couple would have four sons together.

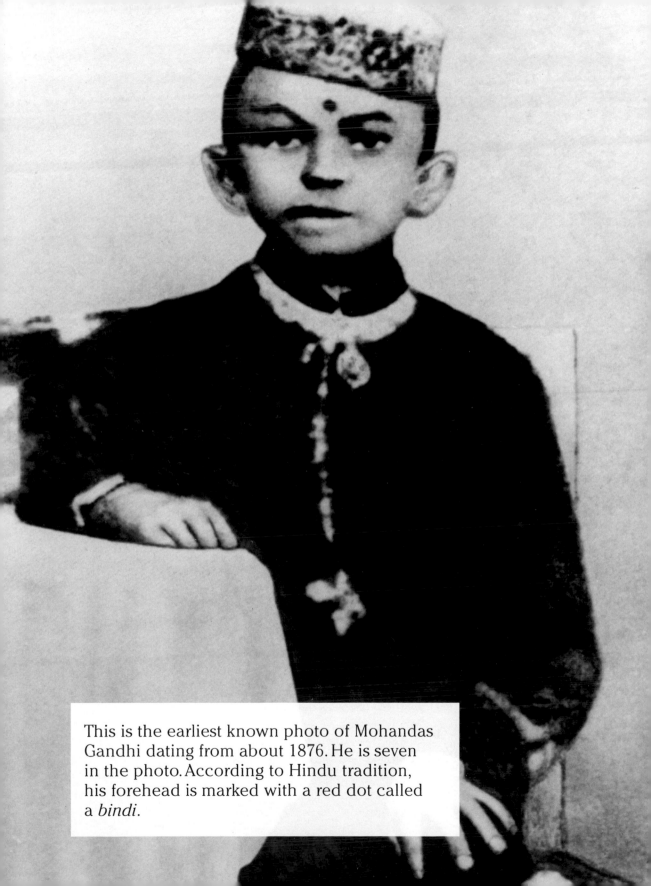

This is the earliest known photo of Mohandas Gandhi dating from about 1876. He is seven in the photo. According to Hindu tradition, his forehead is marked with a red dot called a *bindi*.

A Vegetarian in London

When Gandhi was eighteen, he traveled by steamship from Bombay (now Mumbai) to London to attend law school. He left behind his wife and their new baby son. While he studied to become a barrister, Gandhi struggled to adjust to life in this new, very cosmopolitan city. He adopted Western clothing and manners, but he felt awkward. Adjusting to bland British food proved especially difficult.

Many Hindus practice vegetarianism, and this was true of Gandhi's family. Very few restaurants in Victorian London served vegetarian food, but Gandhi eventually found one. His diet brought him into contact with some interesting people in British society. The rebels, socialists, and humanists that Gandhi came to know included the Irish playwright George Bernard Shaw. In London, Gandhi read the Bible and the great Indian epic poem the *Mahabharata*. The three years he spent there helped to shape the person he would eventually become.

The epic the *Mahabharata* features tales of the gods. This 1755 painting depicts a procession in honor of Vishnu, one of the most important figures in the Hindu pantheon.

Awakening to Injustice

S ad news met Gandhi on his return to India in 1891. His beloved mother had died during his absence. In part because he was so shy, he struggled to find work as a barrister. When Gandhi heard about a yearlong position available in what is now South Africa, he decided to take the job. He left his family behind, once again, and traveled to Durban in 1893. At that time South Africa did not yet exist as a country, and Durban was in the British-controlled Colony of Natal.

Many Indians worked as indentured servants on South African sugar and coffee plantations. They faced mounting discrimination from the local authorities. Shortly after his arrival there, Gandhi had several experiences that drove home this reality. In one case, he experienced the deep humiliation of being thrown off a train when he refused to leave the first-class car, even though he had purchased a first-class ticket. When he arrived in Pretoria, he organized a meeting of his fellow Indians and gave a speech to address these injustices.

These Indian workers are leaving the sugarcane fields in Natal after a hard day's work. South African plantations depended on indentured laborers, who worked long hours for little pay.

THE EVOLUTION OF A LEADER

Though his contract was for just one year, Gandhi spent twenty years in what is now South Africa. During that time, he fought for the rights of the Indian communities there. Whites living in Natal felt threatened by these South Asians, who now outnumbered them. The British government permitted Indians very few rights. They had to pay extra taxes. Their marriages were not considered legal. They were not allowed to walk on public pathways or be out at night without a permit.

While living in Natal, Gandhi continued to speak out against these practices. When the government tried to pass a bill preventing Indians from voting, Gandhi called it "the first nail in our coffin." He drafted petitions against it. The bill passed anyway, but Gandhi's efforts helped call public attention to the oppression of the Natal Indians. Now just twenty-five, Gandhi had evolved into an effective political campaigner.

Fashion can be political. When he came to South Africa to practice law, Gandhi still wore Western clothing. Later, he would give up his suit and tie for traditional Indian garments.

Gandhi (*center, back row*) helped organize the effort to fight discrimination against Indians in Natal. Here, he poses with fellow founders of the Natal Indian Congress in an 1895 portrait.

The injustices that Gandhi suffered made him determined to change the system. He recognized that if Indians in Natal were going to fight discrimination, they needed to unite and organize. In 1894, just a year after his humiliation on the train, Gandhi founded the Natal Indian Congress. He invited both Hindus and Muslims to join, as well as Indians from different regions and social classes.

As secretary of the group, Gandhi wrote many statements about the Indians' grievances. He sent these reports to the press, the British government, and the legislature. He helped call attention to what was happening in the colony. When he returned to India in 1896 to bring his family to live with him in Durban, Gandhi used the opportunity to rally support for the Natal Indians' cause. The British were beginning to see him as a dangerous man.

Loyalty's Cost

At the time that Gandhi was living there, the British and Dutch settlers called Boers governed different parts of what is now South Africa. When war broke out between the two in 1899, Gandhi saw an opportunity. He reasoned that if the Indians in Natal supported the British during the Boer War, they would be granted British citizenship.

Gandhi assembled more than a thousand Indian volunteers for an ambulance corps. The men worked on the battlefields to collect wounded British soldiers, often under enemy fire. Gandhi felt confident that their loyalty would be rewarded. After the British won the war, though, they continued to restrict Indians' rights.

Gandhi was disappointed, but he didn't give up. In Johannesburg, he started a weekly newspaper called *Indian Opinion* to keep Indians informed about government actions and other important news. He read works by John Ruskin and Leo Tolstoy that helped him think about the next steps to take.

The Indian Ambulance Corps, established by Gandhi (*kneeling, right front*), provided aid to the British during the Boer War. Indian volunteers carried stretchers over terrain too rough for wheeled vehicles.

THE FORCE OF TRUTH

In 1906, the British government of the Transvaal (one of the British colonies that would unite to form South Africa in 1910) passed a law that sent shock waves through the Indian community. The Black Act, as it came to be known, decreed that all Indians in the Transvaal had to register. No other group had been required to do this. Every man, woman, and child older than eight must be fingerprinted. The police could stop them, demand to see their registration papers, and search their homes without just cause.

Gandhi urged the Indian community to resist this law. He proposed a strategy called *satyagraha*, meaning "truth force," calling for noncooperation and nonviolent action as forms of resistance. Three thousand Indians assembled in Johannesburg's Empire Theatre and vowed not to register. Hundreds went to jail, but their actions forced the government to offer a compromise. Jan Smuts, colonial secretary of the Transvaal, promised to repeal the law if Indians registered voluntarily. A few months later, Smuts broke that promise.

Jan Smuts was a complex and highly intelligent man. Though he and Gandhi were adversaries, they respected each other. Gandhi once presented Smuts with a pair of handmade sandals.

SPIRITUALITY IN ACTION

atyagraha is rooted in Indian spiritual traditions, though it echoes lessons from other traditions, such as the idea of "turning the other cheek" rather than seeking vengeance against one's enemies. In addition to nonviolence (*ahimsa*), Gandhi's spiritual philosophy stressed the practice of nonpossession. Followers of *satyagraha* believed in living a simple life with very few belongings or material comforts.

In 1904, Gandhi founded a community called Phoenix Settlement, where *satyagrahis* (practitioners of *satyagraha*) could live. They farmed the land, made the food, clothing, and objects they needed, and studied and prayed together.

Though he lived very humbly, Gandhi's influence was growing. His repeated acts of resistance landed him in jail. He organized marches and a coal miners' strike, disrupting the country. In 1910, he established another community, called Tolstoy Farm, named for the great Russian writer, whose work Gandhi admired. The rough life in these settlements helped prepare the *satyagrahis* for the hardships of prison.

This photograph shows Gandhi (*second from left*) and his wife, Kasturba (*in white*), at Tolstoy Farm in 1912. Hindu religious communities such as these are called ashrams.

THE MAHATMA

Gandhi's tactics finally paid off. In 1914, he and Jan Smuts reached a compromise. Among other concessions, the Smuts-Gandhi Pact revoked laws limiting Indians' ability to travel and recognized their marriages. Soon after, Gandhi and his family left South Africa for India.

Two decades had passed, and Gandhi returned a transformed man. Enthusiastic crowds welcomed him back, calling him Mahatma, which means "great soul." They wanted him to lead the movement for Indian independence from British rule.

The British came to India in 1600 to trade but stayed on to rule, despite Indian opposition. Traveling through his home country, Gandhi saw people living in crushing poverty with no sanitation. Most Indians could not read or write. These conditions would have to change if India hoped to successfully govern itself.

Between 1914 and 1918, Britain plunged into a global war. Again, Gandhi wagered that if Indians supported the British war effort, they might help their own cause.

During World War I, one in every six soldiers of the British Empire was from the Indian subcontinent. Indian soldiers were awarded eleven Victoria Crosses, the supreme medal for bravery.

INDIA IN TURMOIL

Thanks to India's support, Britain emerged on the winning side of World War I. But instead of awarding the colony self-rule, Britain tightened its restrictions on Indians. In 1919, the government passed the Rowlatt Acts, permitting India's nationalist leaders to be imprisoned without a trial and tried without a jury.

In response, Gandhi called for a general strike. He urged all Indians to stay home from work and to fast and pray. In some areas, however, the demonstrations erupted into violence. Strikers burned buildings and destroyed railroad tracks. In the city of Amritsar, some British men were killed. Gandhi, the champion of nonviolence, felt responsible.

A week later, British soldiers opened fire on a peaceful gathering in the Amritsar town square. They shot unarmed men, women, and children as they scrambled to escape. The Amritsar Massacre claimed hundreds of lives and wounded more than a thousand people.

Gandhi addresses a crowd at a political rally in Calcutta, India, in 1919 Many Indians were fed up with British rule, and peaceful protests sometimes erupted into violence.

BEHIND BARS

Clearly, Britain would not help India achieve independence. In 1919, Gandhi became a leader of the Indian National Congress and then president of the All-India Home Rule League. These groups demanded *swaraj*, or self-rule, and worked to unify all religious groups behind this common goal.

With Jawaharlal Nehru and other nationalist leaders, Gandhi organized a campaign of noncooperation with the British. They urged Indians to boycott British and foreign-made goods, such as cloth. Some people stopped working for the British, and others refused to pay their taxes. In 1922, Gandhi was arrested and charged with sedition for urging Indians to break the law. He pled guilty and was sentenced to six years in prison.

Gandhi didn't mind the harsh conditions in prison. He welcomed the peace and quiet and the time to write and reflect. However, while he was behind bars, divisions between Indian Hindus and Muslims deepened.

Here Gandhi (*center*) leaves prison accompanied by some of his followers. Years of self-denial helped prepare him for the harsh conditions he endured in prison.

FORMS OF PROTEST

Gandhi's spiritual beliefs informed the protests he organized. *Ahimsa* is the principle of nonviolence toward all beings found in Hindu, Buddhist, and Jain traditions. Gandhi demonstrated that nonviolent action can be a highly effective strategy for opposing a repressive regime. He used nonviolent tactics that included fasting, strikes, and boycotts to achieve his goals.

Many religions advocate fasting, or refusing food, as a means of purification. Gandhi fasted in protest seventeen times during India's struggle for independence. As his health deteriorated, people felt pressure to concede to his demands. After a violent clash between Hindus and

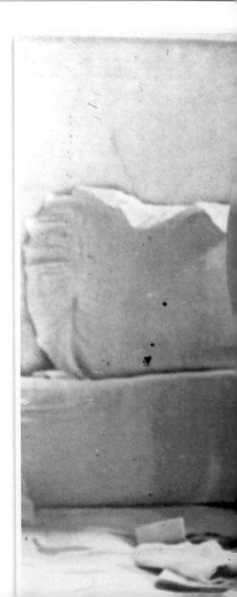

Muslins in Kohat, Gandhi fasted for twenty-one days, until the two groups agreed to set aside their differences.

Gandhi encouraged Indian workers to strike in protest against unfair labor practices and to disrupt British-owned companies and businesses. Boycotts of British textiles hurt the profits of the British cloth industry.

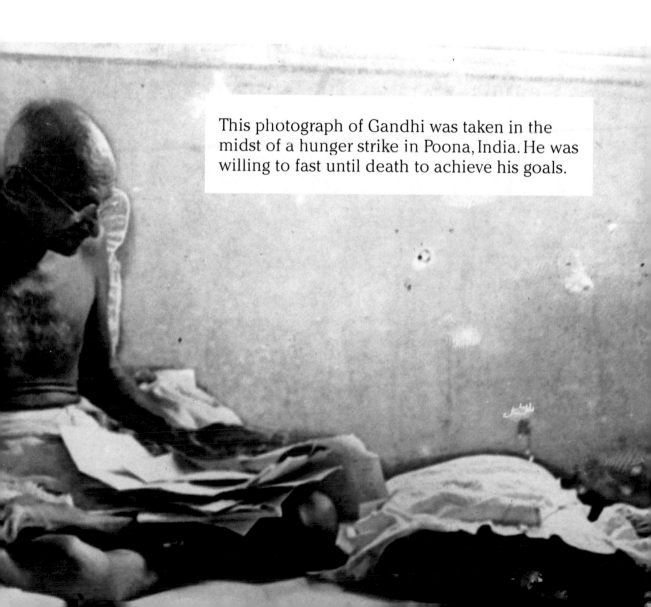

This photograph of Gandhi was taken in the midst of a hunger strike in Poona, India. He was willing to fast until death to achieve his goals.

Gandhi organized the Salt March in 1930, which would become a legendary act of civil disobedience. Salt is not just a seasoning but a mineral essential to the body's health. India

Gandhi and other *satyagrahis* arrive at the seashore at Dandi. Gandhi's salt *satyagraha* inspired nationwide civil disobedience. The British government responded by jailing ninety-five thousand Indians.

had plentiful salt deposits, but the British government strictly controlled its production and sale. Indians who gathered their own salt were breaking the law. The high taxes charged on salt affected Indians from every social class and religious group, which was why Gandhi's plan for the Salt March became so effective.

He and his followers decided to walk from his ashram in Sabarmati to the coastal village of Dandi, where they would collect salt from the beach. In villages along the 241-mile (388-kilometer) route, they would educate people about the salt laws and attract supporters to their cause.

On April 6, 1930, Gandhi reached the seashore, accompanied by thousands of white-clad followers. He bent down to grasp a muddy clump of salt and held it aloft in his fist, saying, "With this salt, I am rocking the foundations of an empire."

THE POWER OF THE SPINNING WHEEL

Gandhi knew that Indian self-rule depended on the people's ability to be economically self-reliant. Gandhi urged Indians to boycott foreign-made goods and to develop cottage industries to make their own products. A family group working from home with their own equipment could produce goods to use and to sell locally. This kept the profits within the community.

With the aid of a small manual spinning wheel, or *charka*, cotton fibers can be spun into thread. The thread is then woven into a rough white cloth. Gandhi always wore a simple *dhoti*, or loincloth, made of this handwoven cloth. He spent time each day spinning thread with his *charka* and encouraged others to do the same to demonstrate the importance of manual labor to the nationalist movement. The *charka* became a symbol of freedom, and from 1942 until 1947 it was pictured on India's flag.

The humble spinning wheel became a potent symbol of Indian independence. Gandhi encouraged Margaret Bourke-White, the American photographer who took this portrait, to spin thread on the *charka*.

FORCING BRITAIN'S HAND

Civil unrest in India had pressured the British government to negotiate. The passing of the Government of India Act of 1935 represented a first step toward Indian independence, allowing Indians to vote for their own local leaders. But World War II (1939–1945) pushed the issue to Britain's back burner.

As part of the British Empire, India was now at war. To prevent India's participation in the conflict, Gandhi launched a campaign in 1942 called Quit India. He wanted to use protests and boycotts to force the British out of his country.

Despite Gandhi's call for nonviolent demonstrations, some protesters destroyed

government property and telegraph lines. The authorities jailed Gandhi and his wife, Kasturba, along with Nehru and other nationalist leaders. In 1944, Kasturba grew ill and died in prison. She and Gandhi had been married for more than sixty years, and he mourned her deeply.

After the Salt March, Indian women began participating in demonstrations calling for self-rule. Here, women protest during the Quit India movement of 1942.

FREEDOM AND BLOOD

By the end of World War II, self-rule seemed within India's grasp, but religious divisions that the Raj had actively encouraged still divided the country. Hindus dominated the results in the first local elections of 1937, worrying Muslim groups. A Muslim leader named Mohammed Ali Jinnah acted to protect Muslim interests. While Gandhi was in prison, Jinnah negotiated with the British to partition India into two separate countries, one Hindu (India) and one Muslim (present-day Pakistan and Bangladesh).

In August 1947, India finally gained its independence, and Nehru became its first prime minister. Jinnah was named the first governor-general of Pakistan. New national borders split villages and families in two. After working so tirelessly to unify the country, Gandhi watched in despair as the subcontinent descended into turmoil. Each group committed atrocities against the other, and hundreds of thousands lost their lives.

Nehru (*left*) and Gandhi (*right*) had very different personalities, yet the affection the two men felt for each other is clear from this photograph.

THE LIGHT HAS GONE OUT

As 1948 began, Gandhi was recovering from a fast he had undertaken to try to unite the country. "I have failed, totally failed," he told a friend as his dream of a unified India collapsed into civil war. On January 30, as Gandhi made his way to a prayer meeting in New Delhi, a radical Hindu man enraged by his efforts to unite Hindus and Muslims fired three shots into the Mahatma's chest.

Violence had ended the life of the peacemaker affectionately known as Bapu, meaning "father." News of his assassination spread swiftly around the world. Even leaders who had once scorned Gandhi mourned his loss. Jan Smuts, the South African prime minister

who once considered Gandhi his adversary, called him "one of the great men of my time." A heartbroken Nehru told his fellow Indians, "the light has gone out of our lives."

Leaders from all over the world joined the millions of Indians who gathered to watch the Mahatma's funeral procession make its way through New Delhi in February 1948.

AN ENDURING LEGACY

Before his death at age seventy-eight, Gandhi fought for the rights of Indians in South Africa and improved the conditions of India's rural poor and so-called untouchables. With a fistful of salt, he wrested India from the grasp of the powerful British Empire and returned it to its people. He strove all his life to embody his moral beliefs and showed the world the transformative power of *satyagraha*.

People everywhere have been inspired by Gandhi's example. In the United States, Martin Luther King Jr. and other civil rights leaders adopted Gandhi's tactics of nonviolent resistance. In South Africa, Nelson Mandela followed Gandhi's example in his struggles to end apartheid, the unjust system of segregating the races. In Myanmar, Poland, and the Philippines, people have used nonviolent action to challenge repressive regimes. In 1989, when one unarmed protester faced down a row of military tanks in China's Tiananmen Square, Gandhi's spirit stood beside him.

Gandhi once said, "First they ignore you, then they laugh at you, then they fight you, then you win." Against all odds, he proved that nonviolence can change the world.

GLOSSARY

ahimsa One of the ideals of Hinduism, Buddhism, and Jainism, it dictates that one should avoid doing harm to any living thing.

ashram A spiritual retreat where people live together and engage in religious activities and meditation.

barrister The British term for a lawyer.

Boer A South African descended from Dutch ancestors.

caste system A hierarchy of strict social classes in Hinduism.

civil disobedience A nonviolent form of resistance in which protesters refuse to obey laws they believe are unjust.

cottage industry An industry whose laborers consist of a family or individuals working at home with their own equipment.

fast To go without food.

Hinduism India's most ancient religion. Its followers are called Hindus. One cannot convert to Hinduism but must be born into the religion.

home rule Self-government.

indentured servant A person who signs a contract (called an indenture) to work for another for a certain number of years, often in exchange for payment of travel expenses and food, clothing, and shelter.

Jainism An ancient Indian religion that forbids harm to any living creature.

Muslim A follower of Islam.

Raj The British Raj, when India was under the rule of the British government.

satyagraha Meaning "holding firmly to truth," or "truth force," this form of nonviolent protest was invented by Gandhi.

satyagrahi A person who participates in *satyagraha*.

sedition The act of encouraging people to break the law.

social class A group of people having the same social, economic, or educational status.

untouchables The former name for members of a low-caste Hindu group that is sometimes considered outside of the caste system.

FOR MORE INFORMATION

Gandhi Memorial Center

4748 Western Avenue

Bethesda, MD 20816

(301) 320-6871

Website: http://www.gandhimemorialcenter.org

The Gandhi Memorial Center is run by the Mahatma Gandhi Memorial Foundation, whose mission is to share information about the philosophy and teachings of the Mahatma. The center hosts an array of cultural presentations of music, dance, art, and literature throughout the year. Class visits may be scheduled.

Mahatma Gandhi Canadian Foundation for World Peace

Box 60002

University Postal Outlet

University of Alberta

Edmonton, AB T6G 2J7

Canada

Website: http://www.gandhifoundation.ca

This foundation's mission is to promote peace and Gandhian principles of nonviolent action. They host an annual conference for youth on topics related to peace and social justice.

Metta Center for Nonviolence

205 Keller Street, Suite 202D

Petaluma, CA 94952

(707) 774-6299

Website: http://www.mettacenter.org

Facebook: @MettaCenterforNonviolence

Twitter: @MettaCenter

The Metta Center provides educational resources on the safe and effective uses of nonviolence for journalists, educators, practical idealists, and activists.

M. K. Gandhi Institute for Nonviolence

929 South Plymouth Avenue

Rochester, NY 14608

(585) 463-4266

Website: http://www.gandhiinstitute.org

Facebook: @ROCNonviolence

This nonprofit helps individuals and communities develop the resources and skills necessary to achieve a just and nonviolent society. The institute prioritizes programs for those between the ages of twelve and twenty-four.

Youth for Human Rights International

1920 Hillhurst Avenue, #416

Los Angeles, CA 90027

(323) 663-5799

Website: http://www.youthforhumanrights.org

Founded in 2001, Youth for Human Rights International (YHRI) is a nonprofit that teaches young people about human rights, specifically the United Nations Universal Declaration of Human Rights, inspiring them to become advocates for tolerance and peace. YHRI now includes hundreds of groups and chapters around the world.

WEBSITES

Because of the changing nature of internet links, Rosen Publishing has developed an online list of websites related to the subject of this book. This site is updated regularly. Please use this link to access this list:

http://www.rosenlinks.com/CIVC/Gandhi

Levinson, Cynthia. *We've Got a Job: The 1963 Birmingham Children's March.* Atlanta, GA: Peachtree Publishers, 2015.

Mahoney, Ellen Voelckers. *Gandhi for Kids: His Life and Ideas, with 21 Activities.* Chicago, IL: Chicago Review Press, 2016.

Malaspina, Ann. *Mahatma Gandhi and India's Independence.* New York, NY: Enslow, 2016.

McGinty, Alice B. *Gandhi: A March to the Sea.* Las Vegas, NV: Amazon Publishing, 2013.

O'Brien, Anne Sibley. *After Gandhi: One Hundred Years of Nonviolent Resistance.* Watertown, MA: Charlesbridge, 2009.

Quinn, Jason, and Sachin Nagar. *Gandhi: My Life Is My Message.* New Delhi, India: Campfire, 2014.

Rodriguez, Ann Graham Gaines. *Nelson Mandela and the End of Apartheid.* New York, NY: Enslow Publishers, 2015.

Saklani, Juhi. *DK Eyewitness Books: Gandhi.* New York, NY: Dorling Kindersley, 2014.

Sharpe, Anne Wallace. *Women Civil Rights Leaders.* Farmington Hills, MI: Lucent Press, 2013.

Walsh, Judith E. *A Brief History of India.* 2nd ed. New York, NY: Facts on File, 2011.

Yousafzai, Malala, and Christina Lamb. *I Am Malala: The Girl Who Stood Up for Education and Was Shot by the Taliban.* New York, NY: Little, Brown and Company, 2015.

BIBLIOGRAPHY

Burns, Kevin. *Eastern Philosophy: The Greatest Thinkers and Sages from Ancient to Modern Times.* New York, NY: Enchanted Lion Books, 2006.

Gandhi Ashram at Sabarmati. "Life Chronology." Retrieved May 10, 2017. https://www.gandhiashramsabarmati.org/en/the-mahatma/life-chronology.html.

Kazuki Ebine. *Gandhi: A Manga Biography.* New York, NY: Penguin Books, 2011.

Kuhn, Betsy. *The Force Born of Truth: Mohandas Gandhi and the Salt March.* Minneapolis, MN: Twenty-First Century Books, 2011.

Lambilly, Elisabeth de. *Gandhi: His Life, His Struggles, His Words.* New York, NY: Enchanted Lion Books, 2010.

Phibbs, Cheryl Fisher. *Pioneers of Human Rights.* Farmington Hills, MI: Greenhaven Press, 2005.

Rau, Dana Meachen. *Who Was Gandhi?* New York, NY: Grosset & Dunlap, 2014.

Saklani, Juhi. *Eyewitness: Gandhi.* London, UK: Dorling Kindersley, 2014.

Wilkinson, Philip. *The Young Protester Who Founded a Nation.* Washington, DC: National Geographic, 2005.

INDEX

About the Author

Monique Vescia has authored numerous nonfiction books on a range of subjects, from social networking to the Emancipation Proclamation. Her life as a nonviolent activist began as a child in the 1970s, attending mass protests against the Vietnam War. She has been marching ever since.

Photo Credits